Travel America's Landmarks
Exploring Independence Hall

by Emma Huddleston

FOCUS READERS

BEACON

www.focusreaders.com

Focus Readers is distributed by North Star Editions:
sales@northstareditions.com | 888-417-0195

Produced for Focus Readers by Red Line Editorial.

Photographs ©: dibrova/Shutterstock Images, cover, 1; dszc/iStockphoto, 4; North Wind Picture Archives, 7, 11, 16, 19; Wangkun Jia/Shutterstock Images, 8, 13; pastorscott/iStockphoto, 14–15, 29; Direct Line Development/Shutterstock Images, 21; Aneese/iStockphoto, 22; aimintang/iStockphoto, 25; Red Line Editorial, 27

Library of Congress Cataloging-in-Publication Data
Names: Huddleston, Emma, author.
Title: Exploring Independence Hall / by Emma Huddleston.
Description: Lake Elmo, MN : Focus Readers, 2020. | Series: Travel
   America's landmarks | Includes index. | Audience: Grade 4 to 6.
Identifiers: LCCN 2019002983 (print) | LCCN 2019004051 (ebook) | ISBN
   9781641859868 (pdf) | ISBN 9781641859226 (ebook) | ISBN 9781641857840
   (hardcover) | ISBN 9781641858533 (pbk.)
Subjects: LCSH: Independence Hall | Independence Hall (Philadelphia,
   Pa.)--Juvenile literature. | Philadelphia (Pa.)--Buildings, structures,
   etc.--Juvenile literature. | United States--Politics and
   government--1775-1783--Juvenile literature. | United States--Politics and
   government--1783-1865--Juvenile literature.
Classification: LCC F158.8.I3 (ebook) | LCC F158.8.I3 H84 2020 (print) | DDC
   974.8/11--dc23
LC record available at https://lccn.loc.gov/2019002983

Printed in the United States of America
Mankato, MN
May, 2019

About the Author

Emma Huddleston lives in the Twin Cities with her husband. She enjoys writing children's books, but she likes reading novels even more. When she is not writing or reading, she likes to stay active by running and swing dancing. She thinks America's landmarks are fascinating and wants to visit them all!

Chapter 1

Birthplace of a Nation

People line up outside. They stand in front of a red brick building. A tall bell tower rises from the building's roof. A large clock on the tower tells the time. This building is Independence Hall.

Independence Hall is a historic building in Philadelphia.

It is the birthplace of the United States of America.

The hall is in Philadelphia, Pennsylvania. It is in an area called Independence Square. Other historic buildings are nearby. The Founding Fathers met in these buildings. These men came from

Fun Fact

The hall became a World Heritage Site in 1979. These sites are recognized for their universal importance.

 American leaders met to form a new nation.

all over America. They worked together in the late 1700s. They were the people who created the United States.

Chapter 2

History of Independence Hall

Independence Hall was built between 1732 and 1753. It was first known as the Pennsylvania State House. The government of Pennsylvania worked there.

 Pennsylvania's Supreme Court worked in this room in the State House.

Pennsylvania was one of the 13 **colonies**. Great Britain ruled them. Many Americans disagreed with this rule. They did not want to be ruled by Great Britain.

American leaders talked about the problem. They met at the Pennsylvania State House to write

Fun Fact

Thomas Jefferson wrote most of the Declaration of Independence. Years later, he became a US president.

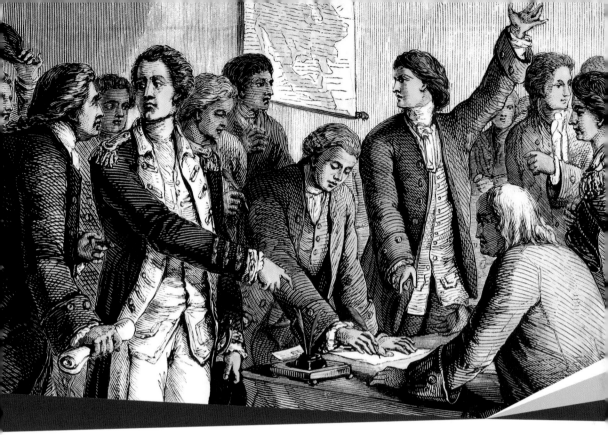

the Declaration of Independence.

It said the colonies were an

independent nation. The leaders

signed the paper on July 4, 1776.

A new nation was born.

Philadelphia was the US capital from 1790 to 1800. During that time, US leaders met at the State House. But the country was growing. In 1800, the capital moved to Washington, DC. Local courts used the State House after that.

In the early 1800s, people gave the State House a new name. They called it Independence Hall. President Harry Truman recognized the hall's importance. In 1948, he made it a National Historic Park.

 The hall's Assembly Room looks as it did when the Founding Fathers worked there.

Truman wanted to honor the place where the nation began. He had the rooms **restored**. They now look like they did in the late 1700s.

The Liberty Bell

The Liberty Bell is a **symbol** of **freedom**. It used to be in the Pennsylvania State House. It hung in the bell tower. On July 8, 1776, a large crowd met at the State House. They celebrated the Declaration of Independence. They listened as a person read it out loud. They heard the bell ring.

The Liberty Bell weighs more than 2,000 pounds (943 kg). In the 1800s, a big crack formed on its side. People stopped ringing the bell. They did not want it to fall apart.

The Liberty Bell is now kept at the Liberty Bell Center in Philadelphia.

15

Chapter 3

Important Decisions

Independence Hall shaped US history. The Founding Fathers made important decisions there. For example, they decided how the United States should work.

 When the United States was first formed, the country was much smaller than it is today.

The Founding Fathers disagreed sometimes. They wanted different things. But they had to decide what was best for the whole country.

In 1787, they created the Constitution. They wrote it in four months. The Constitution lists national laws of the United States. It also lists rights for US **citizens**.

The Founding Fathers valued freedom and **democracy**. Freedom meant that US citizens could make their own choices. They could speak

George Washington (center) led the meetings as the Founding Fathers wrote the Constitution.

up about problems. They could believe in any religion. Democracy meant that US citizens could choose their leaders.

Many important US leaders worked at Independence Hall.

To honor them, a statue was placed at the hall in 1982. It is called *The Signer.* The statue shows a man holding a rolled piece of paper.

The statue honors those who signed important US papers. These papers include the Declaration of Independence and the Constitution.

Fun Fact

The ideas of freedom and democracy influenced people around the world. Other nations took on similar ideas.

The Signer stands outside Independence Hall.

US laws have changed over the years. People want the country to be the best it can be. They can look to Independence Hall for inspiration. They can see its important role in US history.

Chapter 4

Visiting Independence Hall

Millions of people visit Independence Hall every year. They can go on **tours** of the historic hall. People first stop at the visitor center. They get tickets there.

 Visitors gather outside Independence Hall.

Visitors see the US flag in the courtyard. They look at the bell tower. They see the statue of *The Signer.* Then they go inside. People can see copies of important papers. These papers include the Declaration of Independence and the Constitution.

Fun Fact

A silver inkstand is displayed at the hall. American leaders may have used it to sign the Declaration of Independence.

 The Liberty Bell is on display at the Liberty Bell Center.

Visitors have plenty to see outside the hall. The Liberty Bell Center is across the street. People can learn about the Liberty Bell. They can see its famous crack.

The Tomb of the Unknown Soldier is in Washington Square Park.

This park is near the hall. The tomb remembers American soldiers. They fought in the American Revolutionary War (1775–1783).

People can visit Congress Hall and Old City Hall. These buildings are also nearby. US leaders met in all of these buildings. The buildings

Fun Fact

Two US presidents were sworn in at Congress Hall. They were George Washington and John Adams.

1. Independence Hall
2. Independence Square
3. Congress Hall
4. Old City Hall
5. Liberty Bell Center
6. Tomb of the Unknown Soldier
7. Washington Square

have been restored. They look like they did in the late 1700s.

Philadelphia is a historic city. Independence Hall is one of its most important landmarks. It is where the United States was born.

FOCUS ON
Independence Hall

Write your answers on a separate piece of paper.

1. Write a letter to a friend describing the important decisions US leaders made at Independence Hall.

2. Which part of Independence Hall would you want to see first if you went there? Why?

3. In what year was the Declaration of Independence signed?
   - **A.** 1753
   - **B.** 1776
   - **C.** 1787

4. How has the Pennsylvania State House changed over time?
   - **A.** It was given a new name.
   - **B.** It was moved to Washington, DC.
   - **C.** It was made smaller.

5. What does **universal** mean in this book?

The hall became a World Heritage Site in 1979. These sites are recognized for their universal importance.

    A. relating to one city only

    B. relating to one country only

    C. relating to the whole world

6. What does **honor** mean in this book?

In 1948, he made it a National Historic Park. Truman wanted to honor the place where the nation began.

    A. to remember or show respect

    B. to break down or demolish

    C. to make less important

Answer key on page 32.

Glossary

citizens
People who live in a certain city or country.

colonies
Areas controlled by a country that is far away.

democracy
A system of government in which the people have power.
Democracy typically involves elections.

freedom
The right to think, speak, or do as one wants without being
stopped.

independent
Having the ability to make decisions without being controlled by
another government.

restored
Returned to the original condition.

symbol
Something that represents something else because of a
similar trait.

tours
Guided trips through buildings or landmarks that follow a
set path.

To Learn More

BOOKS

Demuth, Patricia Brennan. *What Is the Constitution?* New York: Penguin Workshop, 2018.

Leavitt, Amie Jane. *The Declaration of Independence in Translation: What It Really Means.* North Mankato, MN: Capstone Press, 2018.

Mara, Wil. *Writing the Declaration of Independence.* Lake Elmo, MN: Focus Readers, 2018.

NOTE TO EDUCATORS

Visit **www.focusreaders.com** to find lesson plans, activities, links, and other resources related to this title.

Index

Answer Key: **1.** Answers will vary; **2.** Answers will vary; **3.** B; **4.** A; **5.** C; **6.** A